"Looking is and is not eating and being eaten."
— Jasper Johns.

"Light is not only glorious and sacred, it is voracious, carnivorous, unsparing. It devours the whole world impartially, without distinction"
— J.M.W. Turner.

Contents

Eating the Light

Mary Barbara Moore

This publication won the 2016 Sable Books February Chapbook Contest, as judged by Allison Joseph.

Cover and interior design by Sable Books

ISBN 978-0-9968036-5-6

Sable Books
sablebooks.org

Epigraph Sources

Jasper John's *Sketchbook Notes* is quoted in John Yau, "The Mind and Body Of the Dreamer." Bill Beckley. *Uncontrollable Beauty: Toward a New Aesthetics*. 298.

Turner's note appended to *The Angel Standing in the Sun* is quoted Richard Cohen, *Chasing the Sun*. 358.

Acknowledgments

"What the Sand Says," "The Nineteenth-Century Teapot," "Colonizing Eyes" and "Woman Seated on Stairs" appear in different issues of *Birmingham Poetry Review.*

"Putting on the Glove of Shape," "Amanda Who Is Seen and Not Heard" are in *Bluestockings Magazine.*

"Watercolor Woman" appeared in *Cider Press Review* as did "Venice Beach, 1950" which also is reprinted in its *Cider Press Review, Best of Volume 16.*

"The Looters" appears in *Coal Hill Review.*

"Almost Woman" will be featured in "Hoppenthaler's Congeries" in *Connotation Press and On-Line Artifact.*

"At Second Sight" appeared in *Connotation Press an On-Line Artifact.*

"Eating the Light" is in *The Freeman* on-line, and in the Fall 2015 print issue.

"Metaphor" and "The Principle Of Gold Fish Is the Ephemeral" appear in *McNeese Review.*

"Hilliard and the Queen" appears in Jacar Press's *One.*

"Turner's Sun" appeared in Tupelo Press's 30/30 blog for November 2015 and was accessible through December 2015; that press, however, does not count the blog as a publication.

1.

Colonizing Eyes

The world shows its hand all at once, a spill
of tangerines, mangoes, nectarines,
to the table's wheat- and earth-hued grain,
which ripples the receiving. Even
the straw-gold cornucopia's a sign
of plenitude. We are meant to think:
fruit trees breed for my delight.

Looking, I swallow orbs of orange
and peach-blush-red, puckered
stem-holes, oblation of rounded line
to rounder things. Eating, I fill out.
The caught light anoints my arms
in swaths; I'm oiled and muscled,
cut like circus strong men.
There's no need for stealth, only strength
and health: The world is ripe for my taking.

Even the birds think ripe thoughts,
round-bodied, embowered like fruit.
Magnified, the paint strokes V'd
symmetrically make feathers
like miniature pines. Each small bird
is nearly a landscape! Such orderly
coats of gloss and reverie.

Hilliard and Queen Elizabeth I

Let the world fill with the pleasures
of pleated things: miniatures of royals,
heads perched on neck ruffs
like waves in jewel-colored
enamel portraitures in oil,
and sea views corrugated
in mathematically even furrows,
her mural, the world's glass floor.

Hilliard imagined the colonies like
sea-anemone petals, even barnacles'
huts, both exotic and symbolic.
Dome coral's accrual
in layers emblemed her rule,
like palatial roof-tiles, petals
of bone turned to stone: The world
was seen loyally.

He might have painted little worlds
as her ear-rings—furnace-mouth
red, sea-enamel blue—*imari-*
colored globes. The surfaces would ripple
like Raleigh's neck ruff under the jib
and the half-mast, or the printer
Stubbe's handless ruffled cuff.

No wonder the Queen's pleated collars
attracted the same palette as sea-views.
Each pleat's a ridge, each furrow an abyss.

Whose View

Serpent Mound, Adams County, Ohio

i
The snake's body shapes the path
that rims and mimics the mound,
even the tail curled like a question mark.
It's grassed, crew-cut, the spine
centered like a welt. Who's it for?
The witness's imagined place
could only be sky, but we've substituted
the tree-top-high rickety metal look-out
for the god's eye. From here,
the snake's linked letter S's
look like the creek's,
and the red-tailed hawk
spirals a snake simulacrum
of in and out, back- and fore- ward.
No linearity's here, no stellae.
The lone red spruce is not a spire.

ii
Housing no burials, no bones, toys, tools
like Chuang Tzu's wisdom-yielding trees,
too gnarled, too useless to use,
the sacred mound abides.
Though almost plowed under once,
it's secured now, runic hoard
of words no one's heard.
Handmade in place—of creek pebbles,
yellow clay—it's all torso, footless.
The head's arrow shaped, as if birth
were shouldering upward through
granite burls or ironwood, not earth.

By accident I think, it's near a meteor's
million-year-old bowl, chance overseer
of apocalypse. How things appear
except as falling fears, the snake's speech
doesn't tell. Is it witness or church?

At Second Sight

White-hooded death's head angel, amanitas,
and apricot-colored chanterelle say *Eat us.*
But the Pomos who lived here first knew
both poisonous and edible crops grew
here like Newfoundland sheep wool on wet weather,
like the fog-fed redwoods, which feathered
place's cap. Even now, in full sun or fogbound,
the Bay from air is weird: squid-bodied,
both urban- and wild- sided, its troth
to earth, not man, is clear. It breathes truths
like the light house on Nuevo Año spit
which says: *here's beauty's bedrock; watch out.*
Think of it at second sight: What did Drake think
of rhododendrons and trees whose wood is pink?

Metaphor

Dillon Beach, California

These sheer gelatinous disks evoke
the urge to poke: tear-colored,
wider than a human foot,
their *in* and *out* are all one:
no inward mystery here.
Their organs ordered by fours—
sacs like stomachs or wombs,
something essential—
are joined by pipes of the same
unassuming gray, usefully
redundant.

I avoid stepping on them though
they aren't the same vivid stuff
as me. Senseless, since eyeless,
whiskerless and noseless,
they must be imperiled
making their way through the knowing
waters by feel, all feeling,
guileless, I suppose unless
senses unlike ours imbue
the lachrymose jell itself.

Whatever their powers,
medicinal or venomous,
I needn't collect them;
they're best left here beached
like the sand. Besides, despite
their idiosyncratic concentric style,
their unsoulful (since transparently
mechanical) look, even the gulls
those delecticians of shore orts,
shark chub and whale gut, ignore them.

Here: I can see the sand through one,
its grains not magnified, just queerer,
more opaque. An alien lens.

"The principle of gold-fish is the ephemeral,"

Katharine claimed. They glint pink and bronze,
fan their copper-orange fins. Then they die.
Katharine believed gold fish are sly.
First, they trick you into buying,
puckered lips and bulging eyes,
floating eye to eye, kiss to kiss,
in the commercial tanks. Are they sisters
or mirrors? Either way, they're
like flowers—beauties made to die,
flagrantly.

As you peer, the fish draw nearer.
No wonder you yield
and buy two: the urge to be
reproduced requires contiguity.
Give them porcelain castles and forests
for loyalty, wealth and conquest.
Plant trees of helpful coral:
they bound demesnes and quarrels,
besides helping keep the meadows clean.

The fish then will occupy
water like thoughts, lackadaisical,
fanning, the stuff of meditation.
Like us, they squander days, stake
their lives on children—more
copper scales, more fins that ply
the water like winged sleeves
of courtesans. Geisha-skilled with fans,
they invite spectation at a windowed world.

Imagine their epics, the vincible
armor of bronze and copper scales,
their schools whose law is flowers'.

On the Nineteenth-Century Chinese Teapot

Viridian glaze braided in strands
crisscrosses a yellow ground.
The net of paint and spaces woven tight
catches even fingerlings of light:
it signifies "tree." Stylized rust-red fruit
dot the tree like embroidered love-knots.

Nearby, a figure poises
on a lotus, oak-bark brown:
meritorious, this earthen lotus,
counseling simplicity.

Around her torso
a halo of white glaze laces
the porcelain, the white on white
miming air, the transparent.
She is robed in unpainted
white space, the hair ink-black,
flat, without sheen or dimension.

Everything else frets and is fretted
with zig-zags of gold and what is not,
like the two male figures to either side.
Adorned with thinner halos,
they wear green sashes and gold-flocked
epaulettes, their robes almost papal,
yellow and red, brocaded—
like garbs of gab, maps
of fields and cities, hubs
of commerce and trade.

Hands hidden in sleeves like bells,
they look down. Ballasted with glaze
and accolades, braids
and deeds, they ponder
the porcelain white space below,
the undecorous emptiness
where the only trade
is light and shade.

Eating Light

Collocations, rifts,
brief cleavings and aversions
come and go as air
prescribes—the maple leaves

tap on glass. Translucent,
the leaves shiver and light
tremors on the uncertain
rumors, whispers,

stammers, motions-to-be
signaled in quick torsions
against the window, muscular
flexion of light and shade;

then all stalls an instant
spurning the glass.
The drifter leaves at
branch tips are

bobbing, the inner leaves
held still, deep in, veins up,
eating the light that scuttles
from leaf to leaf

stem to branch, settling
like whimsy itself.
Light's easy shuffle
through leaves' decks

and tiers, its glib
feint, dart and flick,
helps hide the whole
swallowing act.

But if you look and look
you catch sight
of light being eaten:
the leaves shine, flicker, then

vanish; and a house finch,
earth brown, size
of the seedpod it perches by,
settles. Rest

wrested from motion?
Consolation?
A light bead trembles, glints.
The bird snaps it up.

SeaView Lodge

Dillon Beach, California

Though nothing could beat
the blue-black sheen
of the rifles they ran from
in the old country,

the Pacific's glare
would have blinded our grandmothers
whose eyes never met
a picture window's acres.

The sunlight off the sea
bleaches rugs, upholstery, walls.
It lures whatever eyes
and is eyed, even the moth

like a dusty beige star:
it bumps repeatedly
into its mecca, light.
At sunset, the sea coppers.

It stars in a story of stars,
never fixed, always moving.
Is this my mecca,
privileged, incontinent place?

My grandmother probably worked
on her knees polishing
a rich man's parquet
and would imagine

vacations by the sea
and acres of glittering
beach as peace, a panacea.
But what meets the eye,

the shells littering the sand—
porphyry, moon-gray,
moth-beige; horned, crusted,
smooth—are reliquaries death

has emptied of wishful
shellfish, for even the humblest
flesh wishes itself
immortal. The chambered

nautilus leaves her house
there too. Alive, she buried
her eggs in the sea floor
for sanctuary, a cache

of futures.
But my grandmother is with me,
in me. I lift the shell's sanctum,
its insides sleek as titanium,

pink as a kitten's mouth,
a chamber of echoes
and spiralling mirrors, a labyrinth.
I listen, she listens, to a familiar sea.

Light Lures

Likeable sand fleas of light
leap and glint on the beach,
light's charismata,
but even in the deep trenches,
spectral jelly fish luminesce,
their see-though bodies
fluid as ectoplasm,

and now that cameras can sustain
the monstrous pressure
of sight, we can see
in the benthic depths
anglerfish sporting light lures
in the otherwise lampless place.
They're conveniently set
over rows of teeth
like Carroll's cheshire-cat grin.
Their jaws, loosely hinged,
swallow amplitude, awe.

Let's welcome the new chimera
older than Homer, dark-sighted,
who scours the abyss.
Luciferin's the chemical
that lights the photophores blue.

The Looters

The leaves at the window have been looted
pocked with absences   air holes   eye holes
we've eaten more spaces for the light
we're never quite sated by
trees fields oceans orchards in bloom dandies
in suits   we cannot stop eating eye candy
my best royal blue jeans tightening
the noose on my waist   your new shirt opening
little mouths at the placket while Fall's
dry air crisps clarifies spills
ripening apples   leaf piles
bark   my chins wobble   we rock as we walk
nibbling oaks maples   we'd give our eye teeth
for dessert there's peacocks

2.

Turner's Sun

Turner must have hungered
for light's devouring
glory. Even in the forlorn
repros of Nelson's
ship, "*The Fighting Téméraire,*"
eons of fire, of light have turned
the gun ship's prow
beige and white,
into ash, into urn.

Sails furled, the banished
ship fades and feints,
almost mirage,
though it dwarfs the blackened
towboat in the foreground.
Opaque as the coal it burns,
the tug is thick with paint, dense
with what is not light, like an iron
shoe. It smokes, a red brown
plume: its engine
like the sun's is hunger.

At the horizon, low in the painting's
right quadrant, decentered
center, perches the sun.
Arcs of conflagration
rise from it, vermillion,
lead red, crimson—
for it's a star's near fire.

But the disc itself, Copernican
engine, is not red or lemon
or chrome yellow, but wan
as the vanishing gunny,
white as the host
held up at mass: The Christ
of the devouring light.

Chimera

You were panning your camera,
the old-fashioned box with one eye
that's also a nose, black, a chimera
of seeing being seen, but you have suavely done
with it now. Magician emerging
from the black curtain on the back, you comb
your hair sleek as a cap, as the patent
leather shoes I tap danced in.
You've entombed the two palm trees
and me in celluloid. I am so flat now
you cannot enter or disclose me.
I cannot eat sole or poise
for a dive or beach walk and see the sea's
Coke-bottle green curlers unroll in rhythms
of sevens. I'm sheer as your eyes' salt film.

Venice Beach, 1950

I just make out the buoy and the boy
who reaches it, a blond spot at the red
uncapsizeable hat, gone
past the continent's ledge.
He waves. The sea waves too, advances
on a crab's sand-hole hermitage:
inside, it's rimmed with falling
sand grains like stars.
The sea foams, winks closer.
I eye the crab's house.
Will he escape, pincers bobbing,
open like mouths? I pose
the question while my father,
back to the sea, snaps photos.
I am the sea's corsage, a pink
and brown girl, pinned
by unstinting sunlight
to a towel, to the sand.
Sun-burned, hot, I stand.
If you look through me you see
my brother's head bobbing
on the sea's wink and blink.
He emerges, buoyant, beaded, starred.
I am envy's crabbed sister,
my horizon, sand's old glitter.

What the Sand Says

for John Vielkind

The yellow dredges dip plow-toothed heads
in the sea, seeking sand the storm's Hokusai-sized

waves washed away. "Nothing stays or is stayed,"
the dredges say. The sea, unstymied

by gain or loss, stays but doesn't mother us.
It's busier and more Other:

even its borders can't stay moored. If the sea
were maternal, given groundlessly,

a field of waving to yield and be yielded
to, he'd know. He sun-bathed when the red

flags said "rip-tide," and skipped the salt-
froth ropes each wave left in memorial.

They mesmerized him as the stiff gestures
of hermit crabs did, who scurried

and hid in borrowed shells. Sex spread unbidden
from the eyes, weakened knees and tautened

the sodden bathing trunks: he'd best bury
himself in sand, as later he'd learn to marry

or burn, since no one imagined abundance.
Right now, plenitude's tattooed on a man.

He's dressed in artery-blue maps, a world
of fruit- and palm-trees, peninsulas, plateaus.

He inhabits the geography he is,
his torso a mainland, his foot an isthmus.

Nowhere's an island. The man waves. The fence
behind him wavers, its sticks weather-whitened

like storm-salvage from Carolina ruins.
Nearly prone in spots, the fence is sinuous,

staked sparsely as if to stand just so,
facing wind on seaward-slipping sand.

It illustrates the difficult, slip-shod.
Down-shore, the wind in the palms nods,

then cart-wheels inland, promiscuous
touch-and-go caresses;

spins the paper-cup and its logo,
"Pepsi," near the trash-bin; languishes,

then clips the waves like glass row-houses,
snips the cornices, and shears off the tops.

On the sand, each wave produces
skirts of glass fringed in lettuce-white

ruffs of froth. Even the ordinary
taxes belief: seen through the sea's

retreat the sand grains are magnified lazulite,
carnelian, jasper, rose quartz—

a multitude of beauties, not replaceable
as placebos. Plenitude's tangible,

bodily but ungrand, says the sand.

Amanda Who Is Seen and Not Heard

"Love is dead," says the radio talk show host.
Amanda, who is ten, considers this,
but she is learning to tie knots, and sticks
the tip of her tongue deftly to the left
as she ropes a chair to the sideboard's left leg.
Then she reads about horses, while the table
flies with the stairs on the blackened
sky in the window, and the staircase spreads
its accordion light and shadow behind her.
She waits for dinner in the magic, chairs
plush with light, candles flecking
the table's flat skirts like stars. The scene floats
through and behind her on the window.

Amanda abandons her face to the glass,
pupils huge in the candlelight. The ghosts of guests,
dinners and brunches, of parties inhabit
the room: crystal clinks; the heater ticks.
Amanda must be a good girl and should
not speak unless spoken to first. Amanda
minds. She already has dressed to be
seen, her hair a sheen in the light.
But now she reads more about horses,
riding a green world, her hat fallen over her eyes.
And she touches the blackness of glass, leaving
a bouquet of clues, fingerprints, whorled roses.
(But what is her crime?)

She almost seeps into the night, the book
of her face open in the glass, the room
shining through her. But already, Amanda
would prefer to be opaque.
That's why she frowns, her brow
furrowed with the effort of reading
and being unread. Amanda imagines
herself grown, wearing dresses of juniper-green,
shirts of clover-flower white, pledged
to this enduring green, its clouds bulging
with rain, her troth never spoken.
She will lie on lawns, face-up, watching
clouds patrol the borders of sight.

Lovers will peer at their faces in the green
of her eyes. They will imagine her sheer.
But Amanda is the thief of sight, opaque,
and replete with being Amanda.
She will not open the book of her look.

Eurydice

The sun collides with the jagged
pines riding her shoulder:
burning's surmised, but the pines
and scrub oaks only gesture,
traces on the cusp of her,
the crisp of edges
rubbing, tapping, the whole
sprawl hissing, talking.

She shrugs off the golden
shawl of the slope to follow
the footpath through oaks past the creek,
through shadows fluid as thinking
she's yours, sheer like her.

She doesn't do disappearance
but tends away from your desire.
She willows wooded paths
and carries thoughts like lit
water in the flexible
glass of her heart, like childhood,
a jarful of fireflies.

Persephone

The birch shadow composes and loosely
reigns in the red-gold light-shards her skin
throws off. One shadow branch almost bridles
the powers arcing their shoulders inside her,
bristling their lion-colored manes. They are
barely contained. This gives her skin
the effulgence of adobe, smeared with sun.

Some days she is braiding her hair
when I look, two puma-colored ropes she
coils around her head. Loosened, her hair
is lithe and fluid as rain. She shies
away from his eyes, whose corners graze her
with their green. Some of her flies away
at the least touch like a foal; some of her stays.

Almost Woman

The river forms of expectation,
          undulant, mutable, a ribbed
glass streamer distance proffers
          between the lodge-pole pines
at the bend where she might stand.
          She's serpentine and formed
of erasure, innuendo.
          Spruces and red pines ripple
on the shallows
          where the head should be
haloed with these reflections.
          Past nets of tree-limbs cross-hatching
the absence where thighs should be,
          the river descends the stairs
at the falls, unbridled
          and scolding the rock-bench.

What the stones glint to your eyes
          looks like impossible breasts,
but what they become when the amorous
          projection of rock, brow-bone
on the ridge, leans into nightfall
          is anybody's guess.
She almost forms then slips
          out of sight, never become
remorse, dying back into sources,
          earth, water, rock.

Though the viridian
          hair of weeds might fringe
a stone like thought, she's gone,
          or has never arrived.

But the river keeps devising
the places it laves and leaves,
recursive canyons,
gullies, moist traces in the rock.
Descent, its only desire,
the quartz-rich silt
glints in it, a mineral fire.

The Glove of Shape

1

The sea mills tree grist and kelp bulb,
          sorts out its holdings, silt
from sand grain, pebble
                    from glass shard,
but she refuses the spell of shape.

The variegated salt gown
          banded violet and teal, sheer
                    as it falls from
          shoulders to waist,
is the thief of shape anyway, diaphanous
          with boundaries spurned
                    or dissolved.

2

          Your looking cups her foot,
arched with distances and provisos,
          lathes the waist and so
                    narrows her
she is confined, bloodless, an hour-
             glass, the sand grains
          falling one by one through
          the glare, the misprision.

3

Then she ruptures the gloss
          of surfaces, risen,
as from her mother's
          ripe head,
                    into the luck of skin,
to discover wave curls'
          contusion of glass and loss,
                    the skin she is and is in,

the frisson of cold,
        the liquefaction of feeling
inside and outside
        at once.
                Ions of light
dot her and the startled
        cove: she is flecked
with water and the pyrite
        of eye-sparks.

Watercolor Woman

Your thinning hair has the look of wishes.
Even your skin is riddled with white space.
And your arms' flesh-colored wash
is wishing too, to rise and fall, embrace
and release, but you do only the slow taper
toward peripheries, elapse and fade.
Perhaps you already knew as the painter
laid down the fiction, the fear of being
this thin layer, a memory of drifting
into wainscoted walls, claw-footed dresser,
into things, which seemed wholly material,
dense with being. But your intermittence
is like a muscle's fibrillation,
a flickering. It embodies you, like us,
as both endurance and loss.

Cuttings

The jigsaw locust leaves on the glass
play scatter and slash on the floor,
on the Rose of Sharon outside, white
with startle-pink centers
the light chatter feeds.
The bush bobs and sways,
its leaves washing and touching
light, which swells
and retreats, is stayed or let go,
regardless of being seen.

The light touches me too, sometimes
like a lover, sometimes like a thief.
Today, I'm snug in my skin.
Nobody is in me but me.
The leaf-puzzle plays on one arm.
As I lift my arm to open the curtains,
the air slips under, a slight chill,
a quick pressure. I bathe
in the play, the flash and stutter,
and now the swash-buckle sway
of the big palms to the West.
I wash in the cuttings, the difference.
Nobody is in me but me.

Woman Seated on Stairs

Gray oxides of sky, leaf-toothed moon,
Venus's star fritillary white on a notched edge:
you influence it all, the stairs and the door,
the slope to the West, your silhouette
refusing to drown in things. One dimension
is undisclosed. The fourth is resistance
to sidewalks and mortuary columns, and the pure
sense of being singular but more, an aura,
as if skin were the phantom
and jumpy translucence
of flame. It loosely bounds you,
integrating around the spine:
the flexible ivory from which flesh and wish
radiate. The behavior of muscle, bone, tendon,
the language skin distinguishes:
You are these incongruent vectors,
the dicey idea of being human, no omen
the painter might hint at, no dominion.

CPSIA information can be obtained
at www.ICGtesting.com
Printed in the USA
LVHW080412131021
700241LV00011BA/1471